Entrepreneur;

24 Hours To Earn Money From Home;

Methods to run a Successful Business From Home, Running a
Business from Home, Making Money From Home

By

Atacius Hollandbrook

This book is not intended for use as a source of legal, business, accounting or financial advice. All readers are advised to seek services of competent professionals in legal, business, accounting and finance fields.

Table of Contents

Introduction

Firstly thank you for purchasing my book ***Entrepreneur; 24 Hours To Earn Money From Home,*** Methods to run a Successful Business From Home, Running a Business from Home, Making Money From Home.

My name is Atacius and I've been involved in everything from small online business ventures to advising corporate giants in the City of London. Successful businesses doesn't ask you how big you are. Successful Business deals in facts – whether you're making money or not. It's that simple and the business mindset applies to someone making hundreds of dollars/pounds per month as it does to corporate giants turning over millions per day.

Times have become economically difficult and it is not surprising that a lot of people are preferring to stay at home and try to make money from the talents they have. Did you know home businesses that are thriving in today's global scenario?

You probably have a rough idea of what you want to do, the concept of you home business model. But do you have what it takes to get there?

We take a look here at what it takes to create a successful home business model, the things to consider, look out for, and prepare so we can approach the home business with information and make it a success.

Chapter 1: Home Business Models - The Pros and Cons

Let's begin by looking at the positives and negatives of running a home business.

Every business model has plus points and minus points and this naturally applies to home businesses. It might seem very simple to you when you hear about a friend of a friend making a killing working from home. But we need to know the inner workings of running a business from home. We can't judge a book on its cover, let's read the pages.

The Pros of Home Business Models

1. You are your own boss. You could say you don't have to answer to anyone, but that isn't true. You have to answer to your clients, and they are the ones that employ you. However you still have maximum freedom that working for someone else wouldn't afford.

2. You can make your own decisions. You have the ability to take risks and develop things that might be termed unconventional. If you like to think outside the box then being in a home business is just right for you.

3. You don't need huge investment. You could have a whole setup for almost nothing except for a computer, internet connection, a mobile phone and some working space.

4. Not dealing with awkward employees. If you prefer working on your own or just don't like the whole 'office politics' environment, physically interacting with employees then again working from home is great. When you hire people, most of them will be online people, most communication with clients will be done online largely through email and chat.

5. Your own hours – your own effort. You have the capability to push your home business as far as you want to. If you think

you want to stop it at a particular point and start something new, you can do that. You cannot do that, however, with a company you are working in who are extremely rigid. Or expansion restraints could stop you putting more effort into a company you work for.

6. Break when you want. Fancy a coffee at 10am and another 20 minutes later? No one asks you how many breaks you've had or hours you work per day or how many days you work (unless you have that kind of arrangement with a client). You just have to produce the goods.

7. Close to Family and Friends. A conventional desk job would take you away from home every day, including travel times, and you could find yourself barely seeing family. A home business model would allow you to stay close to them and actually even involve them in your work.

The Cons of Home Business Models

1. No one else blame when things go wrong. In a normal company job where you're employed and things don't go to plan, people often shift blame. I wasn't told about this, no one kept me in the loop, I told you to do that, and just a general lack of responsibility. If someone can shift blame generally they will to save their own ass. But if things go wrong with a home business, blaming someone else doesn't count.

2. You have to be knowledgeable about business from Back to Front. You have to know about everything that it takes to run a business, right from setting up your business, to setting up your website, social presence all the way to the other end to invoicing and accounting. Of course, you can obviously outsource all this work, and you should do, but knowing all the things need to be taken care of is vital to success.

3. You have to take on new challenges that you haven't encountered. Creating adverts online, shipping costs, how much to charge for sending things abroad, protecting their securities when you take online payments, providing them support, getting positive feedback and dealing with complaints.

4. You have to be great at marketing. You'll have to teach yourself marketing strategies and tactics. Pretty much all Home business models are operated through the Internet, so you need to be savvy on whether you can handle it yourself or need help. And make the most of it.

5. Dedication to work. Some people lack the commitment to work from home. They lose their work ethos. Restrictions are imposed on people working in an office. They can't just surf the net or get side tracked with a cool youtube video. They keep working and hence keep earning. But at home, there are a multitude of distractions that might happen. Accountability is reduced when you are working from home and you can start something which isn't any benefit to the business at all. You might lose your dedication and discipline for work forever when you start working from home.

Chapter 2: Why Home Business

Let us take a look at the considerations you must make when choosing a home business model.

People often use the term 'home business' too freely. There are in fact several kinds of things you can do from home. Even if we only consider the way people are conducting their home businesses today – through the Internet – there are hundreds of options.

So the question is what kind of home business must you adopt? It is important to know what you're going to go into. What is involved in a specific venture, because without that knowledge, you won't be able to develop the right kind of mindset for your work.

Here are some considerations that you need to make:-

1. Are you interested? Now this may sound like a stupid question but going into a business with one aim to make money isn't enough. You need to have an interest. There are various factors that might interest you. If it is a creative job such as writing or web designing, then the motivating factor for you to join the business is that you enjoy being creative. You might be happy about the way the business operates. You could be captivated by the easy money that can be made in the business - according to you.

What is important is that there has to be something in the business that excites you, will keep you going and driving forward when the going gets tough. Otherwise you won't develop it.

2. There will be various business niches that you can work on. Take the simplest example – writing. You might love writing

and might want to take it up as a profession. Even here, you can specialize, and write exclusively for fitness/sport or something else that interests you. When you are working on what you really like, you will stick with it. After all, this is one of the perks of being in a home business – don't ignore it.

3. Do you have all the resources for running your home business? You won't need a lot of things. But as I've said already you will need a computer. You will certainly need a good Internet connection and possibly as fast as possible. Only that when/if it slows down you're not working at a snail's pace. You will also need space where you can work with peace. Support from your family members is also vital as you'll be working long hours to start with.

4. You need to be driven. Do you have the tough uncompromising spirit? Can you work hard even if things in your life aren't quite so great? The home business will depend on you and only you, and you will also need to be prepared to ask for help.

Chapter 3: Selecting Home Business Models

Let's look at 3 popular home business models that many successful people use.

Freelance Writing and Related Jobs

These have become the most popular home businesses in the current decade. Basically, these are jobs where you write for money.

This can be online marketing, a website or for promotional articles or blogs. There are also other writing requirements involved such as eBooks, press releases, sales pages and more.

People who have such jobs post their job requirements on freelance websites and you bid on whatever you like to do. Some of the popular freelance websites where you can get such jobs are Fiverr, GetAFreelancer, ScriptLance, eLance, Guru, EUFreelance and ODesk. I've used Fiverr a number of times for help in marketing and it's very handy.

In some cases it is not necessary that you actually write. You could actually outsource them to others, and act as the go-between. A lot of people are earning thousands a month just through these assignments.

Pros:

- Easy job for people with writing talents; you can unleash your creativity. You can also learn new things as you write.
- You could see your name on the Internet as an author, but most of your work will be ghostwriting for other people.
- Money comes securely through escrow systems on all freelance websites mentioned above. Not only that you can take only as much work as you want to.

Cons:

- Time-consuming; you earn only as much as you write.
- Strict deadlines to meet most of the time.
- Might get taxing and boring after a while if you keep writing about the same subjects.

Outsourcing doesn't actually seem simple initially, but you are responsible for the overall quality so the stakes are high.

Also people tend to buy on reviews and one bad review could jeopardize your standing.

Affiliate Marketing

There is a lot of easy money in this business if you do it properly. You have a blog or a website where you give advertising space to other companies or webmasters. You then paid according to the number of clicks that you get for your advertisers.

With Google AdWords, you don't even need to have a website or blog of your own. You could funnel the advertisements through this affiliate program so that the advertiser gets a suitable host within the same niche.

Pros:

- There is scope for a significant amount of residual income - money which keeps coming even though you aren't working.
- As your site becomes more popular, you get more income from the advertisers. You can then also scout for better advertisers.
- There isn't much work involved once set up.

Cons

- Not much creativity involved.
- You have to make an initial investment in most places. AdWords operates through campaigns and each campaign costs you.
- Skills with SEO's - You have to have a knack for optimizing for search engines, especially searching the right keywords.

Website Design and SEO

You could get these jobs from the freelance websites mentioned above as well. This would involve:

- Building websites (and managing them)
- Keeping them looking current
- SEO optimization

You would bid on projects that you would like to do and you can take as much or as less work as you want.

Pros:

- It can be very creative especially for people who love creating websites, this is truly great.
- You can earn a lot of money depending on the clients – you can be paid thousands of pounds/dollars for single websites.

Cons

- Time tied up. They are not 'onetime' jobs because even after the website is created, you will be responsible for maintaining it, providing the support, optimizing it for the search engines, etc. However, you could sign a contract that summaries what you will have to do.
- There is a lot of complex work involved.

Apart from these three, there are several other that are popular which you might want to take a look at.

Here are a few names:-

- Multilevel marketing, also known as network marketing
- EBay store operations
- Ecommerce
- Taking online surveys
- Game testing

Chapter 4: The Mindset to Succeed

Once you have decided what you will be doing as in selling or what service you're offering, the next step for you is to start building the right approach. The mental attitude you'll need. These are the things you should think about:-

Confidence

Have a positive outlook. Believe in yourself. You have to condition yourself to be confident in what you are taking up. There will be people who will tell you that this won't happen. Business is full of awkward customers and tricky situations so never take it to heart. Think positively and be confident that you can succeed.

Be Realistic

Set yourself realistic goals. You have to be realistic every step of the way. You have to take up something that you can be good at, and as you take on new jobs you'll see whether you have the requirements met. Don't set yourself too high goals at the start. Be realistic about how your family will react to your new enterprise. They may not be too excited at first simply because it may sound a risk. That's natural. Don't worry though, when you begin succeeding, the support will come as well.

Be Relentless

You have to determined to see it through. Once you've set yourself up to do something don't deviate. You must be staunch in your thoughts. You cannot think of doing something one day with the utmost enthusiasm and then forget all about it the next day. You have to pursue your goals to succeed. The success might be slow, it might come in dribbles and trickles at first, but don't let that discourage you.

Count Your Achievements

Your achievements in this regard however small are important. Learn to appreciate your rewards. Even if they are just $10. It is only when you grow them that bigger projects will come your way. Celebrate even and it reinforces your motivation.

Read

Educate yourself as to how others did it. There's no one way to make it work, there's many ways. Read about other people who have succeeded. Pay special attention to how they fought against odds in their early days. Everyone has done that. Read about how they overcame those problems. This can be great education for you, learn and evolve. Never stand still.

Chapter 5: Things You Will Need - Material and Abstract

You will need a few things to start with your home business opportunity. Without these things, your venture could be a complete nonstarter. Let us check them out.

Tangible Things To Help

- When you are working from home, you will ideally need to create/build a home office. If you can get an entire room for your activities, it is the best thing. That becomes your work place, your zone for being creative and productive.
- Secondly you need a solid and fast internet connection - go for super-fast broadband if you can.
- You might need a printer with a scanner.
- Make sure that the place you are choosing to be your home office is free from distractions. Also try not to encourage other people of the family to come there, especially children and pets who won't understand what you are doing.
- Keep your computer special, which means don't use it for your personal needs such as playing games - unless of course you are working as a game tester.
- Keep it updated as far as possible and have the latest securities installed on it. Old PC's tend to slow down as they age.
- Get your email on your phone so you can reply to customers on the go.
- Remember that your email inbox is the best way to store your work. After doing a little work, mail it to yourself. That way you can keep it with you securely.
- Also remember that everything you spend on setting up your home office is taxdeductible. But conditions apply, as usual.

Non-Tangible Things

These things that are most important.

- The first thing you will need in this context is the right environment. If there are problems and tensions in your house that lead to constant arguments and disagreements you won't get any work done at all.
- Children could also be a potential distraction.
- Working with a supportive family is crucial so explain to them what your plans are, your business strategy, how it will work. Once they understand what you're trying to do, they'll be much more supportive. Make them feel involved. Discuss with them what they can do. When they feel involved, they will be with you.
- Ask for their opinions on things, that way you can gauge a reaction from a customer and also they'll feel even more involved.
- Lastly don't take out disappointments on your family, you need them and this is for them, to better you and them together.

Chapter 6: Motivations

We all have a motivation to make a change, to start something new to make something of ourselves. Things that will keep you going are your motivators.

Having the right kind of motivation is one of the most important ingredients that you will need when you are planning to enter into a home business. It is only when you are motivated that you would be able to follow it through.

Building the motivation?

Failures can be great motivators to succeed. If you have had a bad experience with your previous desk job, it could be great motivation for you to prove to them that you can make a success with this. To prove to them and co-workers that you had it in you to do well.

When you are starting out, there are many things that motivate you – you want to prove a point, you want to earn well so that you can show the detractors, you have the initial fervour that goes with everything that we do. You maybe genuinely happy because you are able to do something on your own steam. This keeps you going. But the problems begin to occur afterward. When you see that things are going smoothly, you might become lax. When you see that there is so much liberty that you can take, you actually start becoming contented. This is when the business starts to decline.

You need to stay motivated. To keep going, to keep pushing forward. And this you can do by slowing expanding and changing your practices. If you keep with the same things you did before, you are going to get bored and won't expand. But if you begin expanding, looking for new opportunities, there will be new challenges to meet. This is what will keep you driven.

Never shy away from accepting new challenges. Try new things, be challenged. When you know that things are going in a streamlined manner that should actually ring some alarm bells for you. You must start looking for new things to do within your realm of business.

Join a social networking groups where you could learn something new about your business or things related to your business. Speak about your work. See if you can get feedback from other people. You will know what people like and whether they are generally appreciative about your idea. They maybe working on things that give you a new idea.

Even associating with new people works. Stagnancy begins to creep in soon in home business models, even if they are paying well. See if there are any day events coming up and book up something. Seminars are great for listening to people who are successful.

Chapter 7: Early Achievements

You want to strive for some early success, to see some forward momentum. That is the reason succeeding early on in your home business is very important. It is so good to see that you have earned $100 in your first week (which is very much possible) even if that is nothing in comparison with your previous employment. The $100 ensures that money will come. It tells you, very poignantly, that if you have earned $100 this week, you can earn $200 in the next week. You then get motivated by this early success.

However we can become too result-oriented. We don't do things if we aren't sure of results or if we don't see results coming in the near future. Patience is a very rare virtue. So we need to keep pushing forward, engaging more potential clients.

If you see people are commenting on your blog posts or articles, people are visiting your website, people are checking out your profile, etc. then it means that you are making some headway. It is these small things that tell you that you are being well-received. In your early days, such response can actually work much better than the money you earn.

Again make it a point to speak with your family about your early achievements. Don't keep everything under wraps. When they will hear about them, they will get encouraged too and they will speak with you and discuss with you. Also if it's not going so well, they may suggest an idea to try that's been staring you in the face.

Your early achievements might be small, but you will remember them for life, even if you will have hundred times this success in the future. You will always remember that first website comment you got, that first feedback you got on your article you sold on ebay, the first review you got from your client on your marketing gig, the first payment you got, etc. Such things help you a lot in the long run.

Chapter 8: Stepping it Up

How do you improve upon the home business you have established and take it to the next level?

If your home business shows some signs of settling down, what do you do next? You have probably grown with the idea that you can make as much or as little of your home business as you want to. You perhaps physically can't do anymore work such as writing. You don't have any more time in the day to produce it. So we certainly need to move forward on this.

Outsourcing

We have spoken about this before but this allows you to do 2 or 3 jobs at the same time. You can hire someone else to do what you're doing. If you haven't used it yet, you must know that you cannot avoid it when you are trying for expansion. You can give out some part of your work so that you can manage more clients, more work and hence more money. Go back to the list I gave you and check out the websites. They're all easy to sign up for and some like Fiverr have a phone app so you can work on the go and outsource while not even in the office.

Automation

There is a lot that you can automate. For example, you could automate your emails by using an autoresponder system. You could automate your website testing by using split testing software. These are just examples. There is automation possible almost everywhere. You have to find out about it and use it.

Diversification

If you're selling something well on ebay, then it's time to try things based around that to step up sales. Things that could compliment what you're started selling or writing. You will have to nurture it just as you did the first one, but with one branch established, you have time to do this. Diversification can multiply your income in direct proportion, but not the investment, because several things will be used in common with your previous ventures. So always keep looking for that new angle to exploit.

Chapter 9: Building a Workforce

One of the main ingredients for a successful home business is a dedicated taskforce. You'll be looking to employ people that you come across when outsourcing. Once you find good people to work with then you'll want to keep a log of who does what so you can immediately go to them.

But you must remember there is a big difference in managing people online and managing them in the real world. When you are working with them online, you obviously aren't actually seeing them. In most cases, there will not be any contracts either. So, how do you keep them working with you?

Giving Incentives

You will have to consistently keep giving your providers good incentives that can keep them working in good spirits for you. Obviously these incentives will mostly be monetary, but they could also be something like a good rating on their website of where they advertise. You can recommend your friends to them. Give them praise for a good job. Also a skype call once in a while is fantastic. You can't actually beat talking with someone face to face – or as close as you can get If they're miles away.

Giveaways

This is for the people who are already your customers or who are likely to become one. Giveaways are important gifts that could help people know what your products are like. This is pure PR and people always love a free gift. Even free ebooks is a great PR move to bring in more customers or to drive them to a website via the free book. They might get a favorable impression from what you give them and really buy your other products. You have to guarantee these gifts are good quality, though.

Chapter 10: Beyond Home Business

Does your home business have to stay at home?

If you find that profitable niche and exploit your skills and talents then a time will come when your home business won't stay a home business. Our perspectives of home businesses are quite old and antiquated. For most of us when we think home business, we imagine a cottage enterprise that works with traditional methods and has a small scale production and a commensurately small income. However this is incorrect, we need to change this impression. Home businesses only start at home - there's no limit to how far they can go.

People who have started building websites from home with just a simple concept in mind have now made their websites global. Huge corporations turning over millions. Hotmail, now a part of MSN, is a very good example of that.

Actually, right from the moment you seek your first client or get your first customer for your home business, you should stop treating it as a home business. You are trading with the outside world. It has not stayed at home. Physical space is in your home, but your business' space isn't. It has gone beyond the four walls of your office.

You must be ready for these things right from the start. You are going to have a global presence, however small you are. Your company name should be on Google, and your goal is to drive that upwards in the search. SEO web designers can help with selecting the best words for you so you get more hits.

Speak with your accountant about the tax matters and what happens if you reach and overcome certain thresholds. Knowing this before you hit them is crucial to maximising profits. Find a PC or Mac technician locally who would repair your computer at short notice. All these preparations have a much greater worth than you might think – they give you a strong indication that your business is going to be bigger.

Conclusion

Finally once again thank you for purchasing my book; **Entrepreneur**, **24 Hours To *Earn Money From Home;*** Methods to run a Successful Business From Home, Running a Business from Home, Making Money From Home.

So after you have read this book, my advice is to mull it over. 24 hours is the title of this book and that's how long it took me to decide to take the plunge in my own business. I had worked out the pros and cons and in the end I talked to my family and said I want to try this. They were supportive and we all went into the new venture together.

So I hope this guide has been of use and given you some insight into how to progress with your business. Tread slowly when researching, but once you're prepared then go like the wind.

Home business as a concept has become more popular today than ever before.

Now, you have the mindset to begin – let's get going.

Lastly please leave a review on the books site, they all help.

All the best,

Atacius

www.ingramcontent.com/pod-product-compliance
Lightning Source LLC
Chambersburg PA
CBHW070310190526
45169CB00004B/1569